# SHR

### Ghos

Prepare to be frightened by these terrifying tales from
around Shropshire

By

Richard Holland

BRADWELL
**BOOKS**

Published by Bradwell Books
9 Orgreave Close Sheffield S13 9NP
Email: books@bradwellbooks.co.uk

British Library Cataloguing in Publication Data: a catalogue
record for this book is available from the British Library.
1st Edition

ISBN: 9781909914940

Print: Gomer Press, Llandysul, Ceredigion SA44 4JL

Design & Typesetting by: jenksdesign@yahoo.co.uk
Front cover image of Stokesay Castle: © English Heritage

# CONTENTS

*The site of the Battle of Shrewsbury is said to be haunted by the soldiers who lost their lives here in 1403.*

# INTRODUCTION

Shropshire is one of my favourite counties. It has a genuine 'olde worlde' atmosphere, with a wealth of historic 'black and white' buildings and ancient castles, nestled among small, patchwork fields which are rarely seen elsewhere in factory-farmed England. Parts of the county look like they haven't changed in a century – and I mean that as a compliment.

As one of the Welsh border counties, Salop – as it is also known – has a wild side, too, typified by high, heathery hills and the tor-like Stiperstones. For centuries what is now Shropshire was disputed land between the Welsh, the Anglo-Saxons and the all-conquering Normans. Prior to that, the area was home to one of the last British princes to stand against the Romans: the mighty Caradoc, who was dragged in chains to Rome and then addressed the Forum in perfect Greek, charming the entire city. The English Civil War also left its mark on the county, and bloody skirmishes and brutal murders carried out during that unsettled time are still recalled in its folklore.

It would be surprising indeed if such a historic county didn't also have more than its fair share of ghost stories. Many of these date from the Civil War and the turbulent Middle Ages, others from the Victorian age right up to the swinging 1960s.

Shropshire's ghost-lore also includes some of the strangest and most dramatic spectres ever said to haunt the British

Isles. Here we have such alarming phantoms as Wild Edric, Bloody Jack, the Roaring Bull, a phantom tiger and a gigantic hand that reached out and strangled a horse! Others, thankfully, are more charming and include friendly monks and maids and a chatty chap in antiquated clothes who paid for his drink in a pub with a coin dating from the 18th century.

The haunted heritage of Shropshire is as varied and fascinating as its history and landscape. I hope you enjoy this tour of its spookiest sites.

*A view of Moreton Corbet, one of Shropshire's many interesting ruins with an eerie reputation. iStock*

## SHREWSBURY'S HAUNTED HOSTELRIES

Shrewsbury is Shropshire's county town, of course, and the second largest in the county after Telford. There has been much debate, not to say rows, over the correct pronunciation of Shrewsbury. Many pronounce it 'Shrowsbury', although these days most residents prefer to pronounce it as its spelling would seem to dictate. The former pronunciation may be a survivor of an early form of the name, 'Schrosberie'. The town boasts more than 600 listed buildings, including a wealth of timber-framed Tudor constructions. As befits such a historic place, it has many ghosts.

Shrewsbury is particularly rich in haunted public houses. Indeed, if we are to refer to two authorities – *Ghosts and Ghouls of Shrewsbury* by James Patterson and *Haunted Hostelries of Shropshire* by Andrew Homer – it would be hard to find a pub in the town centre that isn't possessed of more spirits than just those in the optics above the bar.

The Dun Cow, in Abbey Foregate, is the oldest pub in Shrewsbury, dating back to the 11th century. Its ghost is that most romantic of figures, a Cavalier. Prince Rupert of the Rhine is believed to have stayed in the Dun Cow prior to the Civil War Battle of Shrewsbury, along with several other officers. Prince Rupert is said to haunt a number of places in England, but at the Dun Cow he is the indirect cause of the haunting. Rupert brought to the battle a company of Dutch soldiers to swell his ranks. One of their senior officers got into a fight with a member of Rupert's senior staff and ran him through with his sword. He was executed for his crime, loudly bemoaning the fact that he was losing his life for killing just one Englishman. His apparition, in the full fancy livery of a cavalry officer, has startled people by disconcertingly walking through walls.

More commonly seen in the Dun Cow is the shade of a monk, his hood obscuring his face. Weirdly, one witness described the habit he wears as being 'covered in little coloured dots', but this fails to correspond to any known monastic order.

In Butcher's Row there is another venerable hostelry so proud of also having accommodated Prince Rupert that it is named after him. The Prince Rupert Hotel is of medieval origin, incorporating in part a 12th-century manor house. Inexplicable noises are heard within rooms 6 and 7 and each is described as having on occasions a spooky atmosphere. Room 6 is said to have been occupied by a jilted bride, Room 7 by a jilted bridegroom. Each, in entirely unrelated circumstances, committed suicide when they found themselves abandoned. It's likely that there is one muddled tradition behind both ghosts; indeed the two adjoining rooms may formerly have been one.

The two visible apparitions haunting the Prince Rupert are an elderly gentleman, encountered in a corridor, and a maid nicknamed 'Martha', who haunts a staircase.

*Shrewsbury, beside the River Severn, is Shropshire's county town. Elegant and historic, it is also very haunted. iStock*

A supposed series of suicides have been blamed for the ghostly goings-on at the Nag's Head. The Nag's Head is another of Shrewsbury's medieval inns, and is situated on one of its main shopping streets, the Wyle Cop (Old English for 'top of the hill'). A mysterious painting of a bearded man in a top-floor room has been linked to the hauntings. The painting has been made on the boards inside a closet and is of considerable age, but no one knows who created it or even who it is supposed to represent: an Old Testament prophet say some, a devil say others. One source states that it cannot be overpainted, the creepy face emerging again out of any fresh pigment that is applied over it.

Another tradition states that three people staying in the room have been driven mad by the portrait and have ended up taking their own lives, despite previously being in the best of spirits. One was a soldier on his first night back in Blighty after surviving the horrors of the First World War. Another was a young woman excited at joining her fiancé the following morning. The third was a man who had just been promoted to the long-coveted post of coachman but who then hanged himself in the room the night before he was due to take up his new position. The room is now kept locked. However, this has not stopped something wandering around with heavy footsteps, while uttering moans and muffled sobs.

At the foot of the Wyle Cop can be found the black-and-white splendour of the Unicorn, formerly one of Shrewsbury's most celebrated hotels but now converted to accommodate a number of shops. For years paranormal activity has been reported from this 17th-century timber-framed building. Its best-known ghost is that of a little black cat which, unusually, appears most often in the mornings. According to James Patterson, the author of *Ghosts and Ghouls of Shrewsbury*, the phantom moggie is often seen, and 'seems to be startled by the door opening and so runs from somewhere behind it, crosses the room in full view of the person entering and then disappears through a locked door'.

Mr Patterson also mentions another extraordinary phenomenon observed in the former Unicorn Hotel. He relates that an old grandfather clock was brought into one of the shop units, intended for decoration only, because the movement was missing. Despite having no mechanism, the ex-clock began to 'chime away merrily' as soon as it entered the premises.

At the opposite end of the Wyle Cop, on top of the hill, there stands a grand survivor of the coaching days, the Lion Hotel. Although it now possesses an elegant Georgian frontage, the Lion is 16th century in origin. A Grade I listed building, it boasts a massive Tudor fireplace and a sumptuous ballroom designed by Robert Adam in 1770. The latter is haunted by a shadowy 'Grey Lady', who is glimpsed crossing the dancefloor or standing on the stage. It's possible she is the same ghost, in Victorian attire, has been seen lingering on the staircase leading up to the Adam Ballroom. Another female figure haunts the basement, and a soldier, thought to date from the days of the English Civil War, has been seen from time to time in the bar. Intermittent poltergeist activity has also been witnessed in the hotel. On one occasion, two candlesticks flew up in the air in front of a startled

*A phantom pussycat haunts the former Unicorn Hotel, on the right of this timber-framed pair of buildings. iStock*

housekeeper and on another a door politely opened itself when a night porter approached it.

A Grey Lady also haunts the Wheatsheaf, on the corner of the High Street with Milk Street. The Wheatsheaf was once part of a much larger Jacobean inn, the Riding House. The two shops next door now occupy the remaining space. This equally enigmatic phantom has been seen walking through crowds in the bar before vanishing through an old doorway, long since adapted to create a window. In addition, a ghostly presence, known as 'Bad Tom', is said to haunt the pub. Sudden drops in temperature and inexplicable incidents are habitually blamed on Bad Tom. He has a particularly irritating trick of locking bar staff in a storeroom.

Behind Milk Street is the 15th-century Old Post Office, its name indicating that in the good old days it handled the mail brought by stage coaches. The Old Post Office has several ghosts, all dating from its heyday as a coaching inn. One has been nicknamed 'Lavender Sally', a young girl who sold nosegays to help fend off the stench of horse dung and sweaty passengers. The ghostly blacksmith is never seen but the clang of his hammer bashing out shoes and nails on his anvil is said to still be heard in the pub's courtyard from time to time. The third ghost is much more tragic: a young woman who was murdered by an unknown assailant and then dumped in the cellar.

The Golden Cross Hotel gets its unusual name because it was formerly an outbuilding belonging to St Chad's Church in Princess Street. It was built in 1428 to house vestments and church valuables. Perhaps not surprisingly, the ghost seen here is of a monk. The apparition walks in mid-air, traversing the space originally spanned by a gantry. In the small hours of the morning, the monk (or some other spook) can be heard using an old-fashioned twig broom to sweep what is now an alleyway between the hotel and the church. While researching his *Haunted Hostelries of Shropshire*, author Andrew Homer spoke to a landlord of the Golden Cross who had heard this phenomenon for himself on several occasions.

He told Mr Homer: 'I've gone to the back door of the cellar and it's not the sound of a broom, it's the sound of a besom you hear. I've heard it go from the top of the alleyway to the bottom back door and I've been stood just the other side of the door. It's been that loud and I've flown out of the door and jumped into the alleyway only to find nothing there! I've

*The Wheatsheaf in the High Street is haunted by two enigmatic ghosts.*
iStock

had people staying up in the bedrooms and they've said, "The council are a bit keen around here, aren't they?" They've been moaning about them sweeping the alleyway in the early morning.'

The monk haunting the Yorkshire House, St Mary's Place, is a very different entity. It has been described by one landlord as transmitting a sense of 'absolute evil'. It has the habit of patrolling an upstairs corridor while darkly muttering within its hood.

The Hole in the Wall, in Shoplatch, is built on the site of a medieval manor house, once upon a time the home of Sarah Schutte. 'Lady Sarah', as she is known, has been seen drifting through the Hole in the Wall with a wistful smile upon her face. She is said to have had the misfortune to fall in love with someone who was considered below her station in life. She used to meet her lover in the manor house's stables. Her apparition first manifests where these stables used to stand. The lovers were discovered and Lady Sarah never saw her boyfriend again. It is remarkable that her ghost should appear so cheerful – especially when one source states that she was locked up in a cellar by her furious father and left to starve to death.

The terrible years of the Great Plague are responsible for the ghosts of the Buck's Head Inn in Frankwell. Silently screaming children are said to have been seen and also the apparition of a man feverishly washing his hands as if to rid them of infection. The ghost of the Three Fishes in Fish Street is considerably more charming: a phantom waitress who steps briskly out of a solid wall, carrying plates of tempting food.

13

We are now at the end this tour of the county town's haunted hostelries, and where better to call a halt than at the Last Inn? This was the name originally given to what is now the King's Head, located just before the Welsh Bridge on the edge of the town centre. The King's Head is yet another timber-framed building dating back to the Middle Ages, and it has some fascinating features. During repairs carried out in 1962, a priest's hole was discovered. In 1987, remodelling work uncovered an early 16th-century fresco depicting the Last Supper that had been hidden for centuries behind brickwork. The pub's spookier aspects may be just as old but they are even more enigmatic.

One is a 'cold spot' located in a bedroom overlooking the street. No matter how warm the rest of the room is, this

*The ghosts run hot and cold in the King's Head.*
*iStock*

patch remains icy. In a corner of the corridor outside there is a similar chilly presence. Although some staff are convinced there is 'something' there, they say it never feels scary. Another unseen presence enjoys moving things around in the bar, but this is presumably a different order of entity for it is accompanied by a 'warm feeling' whenever it pays a visit.

## MORE SHREWSBURY HAUNTS

In such a historic town as Shrewsbury, it would be surprising if the only spirits to be sampled were those in its deservedly popular pubs. There are many other haunted locations, of which arguably the most impressive is its castle.

Shrewsbury Castle is a handsome red sandstone fortress, originally dating from the 11th century. It was built by the Norman baron Roger de Montgomery in a crook of the River Severn, a defensive site formerly occupied by a wooden Anglo-Saxon castle. Stone walls radiated from the Norman castle to enclose the town, but little of these remains. The castle was largely remodelled by Edward I as part of his programme to subdue the Welsh but after the English Civil War it began to fall into disrepair. It was restored in the 1920s and now houses the Shropshire Regimental Museum.

During the 900s, a tyrant was in command of the Anglo-Saxon castle. Due to his murderous habits, he is known to tradition as 'Bloody Jack'. This villain was a kind of Dark Age Bluebeard, a cruel sadist who would lure young women to his castle in order to torture and eventually murder them. The victims' dismembered bodies were dumped in the Severn. The townspeople could only put up with so much and when a merchant's pretty daughter vanished from the marketplace, Bloody Jack's days became numbered. The merchant made his way up to the castle, in the company of a sympathetic band of other town worthies, ostensibly to ask for help in finding her. Rumours had already reached his ears regarding Jack's excesses, however, and he strongly suspected that he would find his daughter within the castle's walls.

Shortly after demanding entrance to the castle, the merchant and his companions heard cries for help. The merchant's daughter came flying out of a door, her clothing torn, her long hair streaming behind her. She had made the best of the confusion caused by her father's appearance to make her escape. The rough treatment the girl had received at the hands of Bloody Jack and his men was self-evident and there was little need for her to explain what had befallen her. Here at last was the evidence the townsfolk of Shrewsbury had needed to rise up against their lord.

The townspeople raided the castle. In Jack's bedchamber they made one particularly gruesome discovery: a box containing the snipped-off fingers and toes of eight victims, each set neatly bound in a strip of cloth ripped from their dresses. Everyone in the castle was rounded up but the murderer himself was not among them. A diligent search found him hiding up a chimney. He was dragged out and, according to tradition, hanged, drawn and quartered on the Wyle Cop. Afterwards his head was stuck on a spike for all to see.

Bloody Jack is now said to haunt the castle, a grim and forbidding spectre. Another ghostly relic of this horror is the apparition of a girl which runs screaming towards the gates from a tower in the grounds, called Laura's Tower. This is either the ghost of one of Jack's victims or that of the merchant's daughter making her escape.

*Shrewsbury Castle is haunted by the murderous Bloody Jack.*
*iStock*

On stormy nights, a party of people in medieval costume have been seen making their uncertain way towards Shrewsbury Castle. The apparition recalls an event which took place a century after Bloody Jack's infamous career. By this time the Norman castle had been built and Roger de Montgomery was in charge of it.

In the south of the county, near Bridgnorth, Adelaide (or Adeliza), the sister of William the Conqueror, was caught in a violent storm and she and her party began to fear for their safety. Adelaide prayed for deliverance and experienced a vision in which she was told that if she built a religious house where she was now kneeling, she would be spared. Emboldened by this promise from above, Adelaide and her companions struggled on to Shrewsbury in order to report to Roger – himself a notably religious man who had already founded a monastery – for permission to comply with the heavenly command. St Mary Magdalene's Church at Quatford is on the site of the religious community founded by Adelaide after her safe delivery.

On the outskirts of the town is the site of the Battle of Shrewsbury, fought in 1403. This is where the forces of King Henry IV clashed with those of the rebellious Duke of Norfolk. It was a fearsome scrap and the field was said to have afterwards lain four bodies deep. Henry Tudor was victorious, however, and the battle helped cement his reign, after taking the throne from Richard II. Spectral soldiers have been seen creeping across the battlefield, as if trying to escape the carnage that took place all those centuries ago.

Shrewsbury Castle overlooks the town's splendid Victorian railway station. Platform 3 is haunted by a local councillor who died while waiting for a train in the 1880s. It was the depths of winter and his train had been delayed by a blizzard. It had been snowing for days, so much so that the weight of its accumulation was too much for the shelter's cast-iron and glass roof. The glass shattered and the entire structure, plus snow, came crashing down onto the unfortunate man's head. His ghostly form is said to still be seen, glancing anxiously at his pocket watch or vainly peering up the line for the train that arrived fatally late.

In the middle of town can be found the magnificent half-timbered mansion known as Rowley's House. It formerly housed Shrewsbury's museum but is now the office of the tourist information centre. One of its purported ghosts may now have moved on, for it was intimately linked with a museum exhibit. She would be seen, in the elaborate costume of a past century, stretched out on a four-poster bed. It has been suggested that she died in childbirth on the bed. Assuming that this artefact is now to be found in the new museum in Shrewsbury's long-defunct music hall, the ghostly lady may well have gone with it. Rowley Hall's other ghost has often been encountered wandering the corridors. The shadowy male figure is surrounded by an aura of peace, but his appearance is too indistinct to accurately identify him or the period to which he belongs.

Even older than Rowley's House is the building now occupied by the WH Smith store on Pride Hill: it began life as the home of the Pride family in the 1200s. The face of a sorrowing girl is said to stare out of an upper-storey window. She has been nicknamed 'Bertha' and appears to be looking over to the Pride Hill Cross, which marks the site of Shrewsbury's scaffold. Was Bertha watching an execution centuries ago, perhaps of someone she loved?

*An unfortunate passenger haunts Platform 3 at Shrewsbury's impressive railway station. iStock*

Shrewsbury has been a market town since before the Norman Conquest. King's Market was the original venue but in the 13th century the more spacious Market Square was created. Its Elizabethan Market Hall is a striking feature of the square and is said to be haunted by a child who died during its construction. One of its heavy beams slipped out of the haulage gear and crushed the little girl to death. James Patterson, author of *Ghosts and Ghouls of Shrewsbury*, was a policeman before he took up his pen. As a bobby on the beat, he had an eerie experience in Market Square. He recalls:

'Once when I was a constable on night duty I walked and walked my beat, doubling back again and again. I could hear a child crying constantly and knew something was amiss. The crying carried on for at least two hours – as did my fruitless search. I never seemed to get any closer to the noise.'

At the time he knew nothing of the ghost. Mr Patterson had one other, even spookier experience during his time as a Shrewsbury copper. It occurred in Barracks Passage, a narrow alleyway off the Wyle Cop. Here young PC Patterson saw something he described as 'a shape'. 'It was about four feet high,' he writes, 'and completely covered from head to toe in a rough woollen cowl of the type used by monks. Only this cowl had no holes for the eyes or arms and no feet protruded from the bottom. I got the impression it may have been female but there were no identifying features except to say that this creature exuded absolute evil.'

This alleyway – or 'shut' as they are known in Shrewsbury – had an eerie reputation but no explanation has ever been forthcoming for the malignant 'shape'. Many of

*Shrewsbury's Market Square, where author James Patterson had a decidedly eerie experience. iStock*

Shrewsbury's shuts are haunted and so too are many other locations, all of them detailed in Mr Patterson's fascinating book.

## THE OTHER HAUNTED TOWNS

In 1995 a photograph was presented to the public which became celebrated as one of the most authentic ever taken of a ghost. The photograph was taken by Mr Tony O'Rahilly during a disastrous fire at Wem Town Hall. Mr O'Rahilly, who lived in Wem, was on the scene shortly after the blaze began. The photo shows what appears to be the face and upper body of a young girl standing among the flames, apparently wearing a belted gown and staring out of the fire with a solemn expression.

The photograph was examined by experts and pronounced to be genuine. Clearly, no real person could be standing in the midst of such a blaze. However, it was conceded that some combination of light and shadow cast by the flames might have created the simulacrum of a girl, albeit an extraordinarily realistic one. Soon after the photo was printed in the British media, a story surfaced that an older town hall on the same site had burned down in 1677, the fire caused by a girl called Jane Churm knocking over a candle. The photograph now became more compelling. Did it show Jane's spirit? Had the fire brought her back from the grave? Could her ghost have been responsible for the 1995 disaster?

For fifteen years the Wem Town Hall ghost photo remained one of the most talked about and, with the increased accessibility of the internet, the most viewed. However, in 2010, Shrewsbury resident Brian Lear was examining a postcard of Wem High Street taken in 1922 when he spotted a girl in the same pose and wearing the same outfit as the Town Hall 'ghost' standing in the street. The postcard had been reproduced in the nostalgia section of his local paper. The 1922 girl and the alleged ghost are so similar that many now believe Mr O'Rahilly must have used a copy of the same postcard to create the ghost using a double exposure process. Mr O'Rahilly passed away in 2005 so he is unable to either defend himself or own up to a clever and captivating hoax. The Wem ghost photo will therefore remain an intriguing mystery.

Telford is the largest town in Shropshire and was created in the 1960s and 1970s. Despite its modernity, there are one or two haunts on record from the days before the housing estates were built.

The play area in the Brookside housing estate is haunted by a man with a Jack Russell dog. He has been known to shake his fist and shout at children to 'get off his land'. That he is no mortal man was proved when a gang of outraged kids decided to take him to task. They followed him as he passed from view behind an oak tree. They rushed round but found that both man and dog had vanished. Moments later they heard *from behind them* the angry demand of 'Get off my land!' The irate gentleman was now standing in the middle of the playing area, where he had somehow transported himself in a matter of seconds without being seen. Presumably he is the ghost of a farmer who used to own the land before it was developed.

*Ghostly echoes of the past have been witnessed in the modern new town of Telford.*
iStock

By far the strangest ghost reported from the suburbs of Telford is the Ketley tiger. Allan Scott-Davies recounts the story behind this extraordinary spook in his *Haunted Shropshire*. He explains that the now long-gone village green had been the setting of popular May Day celebrations and annual visits by a circus. Many years ago, two schoolboys sneaked into the off-limits area behind the big top and were soon drawn to the cage where an enormous tiger was sleeping. They decided to wake it up – and began to poke it with a stick. The effect was hardly surprising. The savage animal did indeed wake up and began to pace its cage. But this was not enough for the two boys; they wanted to make it roar. So they began to torment it further with shouts and jeers.

Eventually, the infuriated tiger leapt at the two boys, grazing the arm of one of them. Tasting blood, it hurled itself at the bars a second time, with more force than before. It was unable to break through the solid steel to reach its tormentors but, tragically, broke its neck in the attempt. The boys ran away, leaving the majestic beast dead in its cage.

Roads now cover the green and, according to Mr Scott-Davies, amazed motorists have seen a tiger pacing an invisible cage on a traffic island. It snarls, leaps into the air – and vanishes.

In 1905 an exciting discovery was made beside a new road leading out of Brynhafod Lane in Oswestry. When the road was under construction workmen uncovered a hoard of more than 400 gold and silver coins dating from the reign of Henry VIII up to that of Charles I. As far as could be determined, the coins were hidden in 1643, when the English Civil War was gaining momentum, plunging the nation into uncertainty and strife. Rumour had it that for many years a ghost had haunted the spot where the treasure was found. Traditional ghost-lore insists that people would be doomed to haunt the place they had hidden any valuables until they came to light.

A classic work on the supernatural, *The Night Side of Nature*, first published in 1848, describes another haunting in Oswestry. The author, Catherine Crowe, learnt of the ghost from 'the daughter of the celebrated Mrs S'. Lady C. Milnes Gaskell, in *Friends Round the Wrekin* (published in 1914), identifies 'Mrs S' as 'Mrs Siddons', presumably the famous actress of the Georgian period. Catherine Crowe explains that the lady and her husband were travelling into Wales and decided to stay for a few days in Oswestry. She continues:

'There they established themselves in a lodging, to reach the door of which they had to go down a sort of close or passage. The only inhabitants of the house were the mistress, a very handsome woman, and two maids. Mr and Mrs S, however, very soon had occasion to complain of the neglected state of the rooms, which were apparently never cleaned or dusted; though, strange to say, to judge by their own ears, the servants were doing nothing else all night, their sleep being constantly disturbed by the noise of rubbing, sweeping and the moving of furniture.

'When they complained to these servants of the noise in the night, and the dirt in the rooms, they answered that the noise was not made by them, and that it was impossible for them to do their work, exhausted as they were by sitting up all night with their mistress, who could not bear to be alone when she was in bed. Mr and Mrs S afterwards discovered that she had her room lighted up every night; and one day, as they were returning from a walk, and she happened to be going down the close before them, they heard her saying, as she turned her head sharply from side to side, "Are you there again? What the devil! Go away, I tell you!" etc. etc.

'On applying to the neighbours for an explanation of these mysteries, the good people only shook their heads, and gave mysterious answers. Mr and Mrs S afterwards learned that she was believed to have murdered a girl who formerly lived in her service.'

A contributor to an Oswestry-based journal, *Bye-gones*, spoke to an elderly resident, who was familiar with this house but unfortunately did not share the location with her readers. Her informant told her: 'It was a little dingy house that looked west, and had a lot of winders [*sic*], but none of 'em seemed to give any light.'

She added the rather splendid comment: 'It was a house of master-crime.' We also learn that it was destroyed by fire in about the 1870s and that by the time the *Bye-gones* article appeared 40 years later, where it had stood nothing but weeds would grow.

*A phantom tiger is undoubtedly one of Shropshire's strangest ghosts.*
iStock

Whitchurch, despite being a town of great age and interest, only appears to have one haunted location and it's a surprisingly modern one. This is the Civic Centre, where the ghostly strains of a piano have been heard after dark. The music has been heard even after the building has been locked up for the night. Security guards have been unable to track down the source of the tinkling ivories.

Another municipal building, the Clock Tower in Shifnal, is also possessed of an enigmatic ghost. From time to time a strange white figure has been seen jumping up in front of the clock face. It is thought this might be the spirit of the man who originally put up the money to have it built, an autocratic businessman who wanted to make sure no one in Shifnal had an excuse for being late for work. The project proved more expensive than he'd anticipated, however, and when he fell ill the donor demanded that work stop on the half-completed Clock Tower. The townspeople clubbed together after his death to complete what would otherwise have been an unfinished eyesore. Tradition has it the businessman's spirit was annoyed by this and every now and then it returns to try to interfere with the clock or to block people from seeing the time.

Ludlow is one of Shropshire's most beautiful towns and has no fewer than 500 listed buildings. Although Shrewsbury has the greatest number of haunted hostelries, Ludlow can boast arguably the handsomest. The 16th-century Feathers Hotel is a picture-book perfect confection of timbers, leaded windows and wonky floor levels. It has a haunted bedroom in which all manner of peculiar goings-on have been reported by guests. One couple watched open-mouthed while something invisible opened the wardrobe and chucked all their clothes onto the floor. Others have felt icy, disembodied fingers raking down their back. Another weird phenomenon is the sound of applause followed by hurrying footsteps. What they signify is anyone's guess.

In 1974, a travelling salesman had just parked outside the Feathers when a young woman caught his eye. She looked very attractive in her miniskirt and flimsy blouse, so the man barely noticed her out-of-date fashion sense as she strolled across the road towards him. However, he got a serious shock when she walked straight through his parked car as if it wasn't there and then continued nonchalantly on her way! He recovered his senses sufficiently to crawl to the Feathers' bar and order a large scotch. He learnt from the barman that the mini-skirted phantom had been seen by a number of other witnesses. One researcher identified the ghost as a woman who used to visit her aunt in Ludlow in the 1960s. This woman, however, was still very much alive, merely ten years older.

There are at least two more haunted old inns in Ludlow. The Bull is one of the oldest buildings in the town. It is haunted by an elderly woman of uncertain identity and another presence (or perhaps the same one) that has the unnerving habit of grasping people by the shoulder. Those affected will turn to find no one visible behind them.

The Globe, near the castle, is now a wine bar and Thai restaurant. At one time it was patrolled after dark by the apparition of an elderly man in a nightshirt. He would shuffle down a corridor carrying a lighted candle in a brass candlestick. A woman who saw him late one December night in 1916 recalled the 'long wisps of white hair' peeping out from under his nightcap. She had been on the way to the loo, when a door opened and the man wandered out. Embarrassed at being seen in her nightie, she blurted out: 'Who are you?' The ghost genially replied: 'It's only me,' before shuffling off into the darkness.

Guests in the Globe also reported seeing the ghosts of a man in a cloak 'who had his hair tied behind' and another wearing a leather jerkin and a medieval helmet. Sometimes they are seen together. It has been suggested that one of them is Edward Dodson, a soldier who was murdered in his bed here in the 16th century.

There is also a story of a little, amiable chap who erupted into the bar one evening, dressed in old-fashioned clothing. He ordered a sherry and told the barman that his coach had been delayed and that he would have to shelter in the Globe for a little while. He then sat by the fire and wittered on about the perils and inconveniences of travelling by night. At 8pm the door blew open and the stranger hurried out, wishing everyone a hasty good night. The rattle of horses' hooves on cobbles and the creaking of leather was heard as a coach-and-horses apparently drove away. Only now did the people in the bar begin to wonder about the odd little interloper. It dawned on them that they'd been in a kind of trance. The barman was more concerned that he hadn't paid for his drink. But then he found a little coin lying on the bar. He picked it up and was amazed to see it was dated 1765.

*The Feathers Hotel in Ludlow is one of England's best-known inns. A number of guests have had spooky experiences here. iStock*

It is not just the inns that are haunted in Ludlow; you may encounter ghosts in the street. A woman named Sheppard had an eerie experience in Corve Street, as related by Christine McCarthy in her *Some Ghostly Tales of Shropshire*.

'In front of me was a refined-looking gentleman wearing the style of clothing associated with the caricature of John Bull,' recalled Miss Sheppard. 'He was hurrying towards St

31

Leonard's Chapel, hesitated and suddenly faded away on reaching the burial ground. There was nothing frightening about the figure, or his vanishing. It was just puzzling.'

Christine McCarthy adds that spectral monks have also been seen in Corve Street. The town's mighty medieval castle has its ghosts, too. The best-known is Marion de Bruyere, whose father was custodian of Ludlow Castle during the reign of King Henry II. Marion had a secret lover, whom she would smuggle into her chamber by lowering a rope over the castle walls. Marion was left alone at the castle for a spell while her father was away fighting. It was then that she made the shocking discovery that her lover was a traitor who had just been using her to gain access to the castle. One night, while Marion was enjoying a bath, he sneaked in with a gang of armed men, who overpowered the guards. When Marion discovered what was happening, she was, of course, distraught but, being a girl of her time, she didn't waste time in tearful recriminations; she took revenge by grabbing her treacherous suitor's sword and running him through with it. She then threw herself to her death from the battlements.

Such a strong and tragic personality is just made for a ghost story. Marion's restless spirit is said to haunt the place where she took her own life, the so-called Hanging Tower. However, she may not be the only phantom female haunting Ludlow Castle. A unique manuscript discovered a hundred years ago in a locked drawer in a local house refers to 'a pale lady' who used to manifest in one of the bedrooms. The account, written down in rather poor verse, describes the apparition as standing in front of an old mirror, rending her hair and wringing her hands. The poem makes it clear she was killed by her lover, rather than the other way round, so she cannot be Marion de Bruyere. It would appear, too, that her appearances were omens of death:

'She comes with the midnight; – meet not her cold eye; –
It shines but on those who are fated to die.'

Over in Much Wenlock, a handsome half-timbered building near the church is haunted by laughing children of a past age, playing with a spinning top. The town's George and Dragon pub has two related ghosts, a friendly black dog which died of the ill-treatment it suffered at the hands of a former landlord and the quiet sobbing of the barmaid who had loved it. Disembodied footsteps heard in one of the town's shops are believed to belong to a chemist who drank

*Two spectral ladies haunt Ludlow Castle. Both have tragic tales, involving traitorous lovers. iStock*

a cocktail of gin and arsenic after accidentally prescribing the wrong drug to a child, who died as a result. In Market Drayton a similar phenomenon was heard in the Corbet Arms Hotel, and was said to belong to the unhappy spirit of a chambermaid who hanged herself in despair after being jilted at the altar.

After Shrewsbury, Bridgnorth must be the most haunted town in Shropshire. In common with its neighbours, it has numerous inn spectres. The Black Boy is haunted by a woman in a blue dress; the Falcon by a former 'regular' known as Willie; the Crown by an 18th-century servant called 'Evie', who likes to move things about and whose footsteps are frequently heard; and the Holyhead Hotel by a shadowy male figure, the scent of perfume and a mysterious clicking noise.

The old pub and restaurant known as Magpie House (and more recently as the Bassa Villa) stands on the Cartway, a historic street connecting Low Town with High Town. A tragedy occurred here in the 17th century. Two children were playing hide and seek in the cellar and were inadvertently locked in. The River Severn was in flood at the time and when it unexpectedly burst its banks, the water swept into the cellar, drowning the little ones. Their voices are said to still be heard, crying vainly for help. The ghost of their bereaved mother, dressed in the deepest mourning, also haunts the house.

The 'Woman in Black' who was seen by two policemen walking down the High Street before turning into the Cartway may possibly be the same ghost. The officers described her as being tall, good-looking but with a 'pale waxy face' and wearing a long black cape and lace-up boots. Because it was very late at night, they asked her if she was 'all right' and she replied, 'Yes, thank you.' The policemen saw the woman on four different nights, always in the small hours of the morning and always in the same place. On each occasion she would vanish from view with mysterious rapidity and it began to dawn on them that this was no earthly woman.

After the story of the Woman in Black reached the local newspapers, a journalist named Brian Hill lay in wait for her late one night and claimed to have met and spoken with her. She told him his name, before gliding away into the darkness. Like the mini-skirted ghost of Ludlow, Mr Hill believes she

*In Bridgnorth's historic Cartway two ghostly women in black have been encountered – or possibly the same one in two different locations. iStock*

was the ghost of a woman still living in Bridgnorth, but of her much younger self. He never revealed the name of this woman. Another theory, suggested by a local historian, is that she is the ghost of a woman who had committed suicide near the same spot after a love affair was broken off.

A friendly spook called 'Old Mo' has frequently been met with in an area along the bank of the River Severn. Old Mo was a monk belonging to Bridgnorth's medieval Franciscan Friary, which was situated between the river and Friar's Street. The Franciscans were a devout and humble order and Old Mo didn't suit them at all. He enjoyed a drink and the company of women and would frequently go AWOL from the friary to enjoy the delights of the medieval town. Concerned that he was ruining their reputation, a gang of his angry brothers committed the decidedly un-Christian act of poisoning him. Old Mo's hooded form was most often seen in the incongruous setting of a carpet factory (demolished in the 1980s) which was built on the site of the friary. A spectral monk seen in the Acton Arms in nearby Morville is also said to be Old Mo.

Only a fragment – and an amusingly wonky one at that – survives of Bridgnorth Castle. This is hardly surprising, for it was blown up by the Parliamentarians during the Civil War. Its ghost is thought to date from this violent period in British history, but since it is invisible this cannot be known for sure. The sound of hooves galloping on a cobbled surface is followed by footsteps running into the ruin. This is believed to be the ghostly echo of a despatch rider's frantic efforts to warn the Royalist garrison of the approaching Roundhead army.

The spooky activity reported from St Leonard's Church is also heard not seen. The church organ has been known to play itself. A couple visiting one Saturday morning heard organ music emanating from the church as they approached, and it continued even while they were walking round inside. It was only when the man happened to glance over at the organ itself that the music suddenly ceased. He saw to his amazement that there was no one sitting at the instrument.

The nearby St Leonard's Steps may also be haunted. Some years ago a resident met an elderly lady on the steps, whom Christine McCarthy describes as wearing 'old-fashioned clothes, including lace-up boots and a black hat which was adorned with imitation cherries'. She was also carrying a large basket over her arm. The witness spoke a few words to

*An invisible horse has been heard galloping towards the wonky remains of Bridgnorth Castle. iStock*

the woman, puzzled that she should be about at three in the morning. Describing his encounter to friends some time later, he was told that the woman he had described closely resembled someone who had died many years ago.

Bridgnorth's railway station dates from the 1860s and was closed down a hundred years later. Fortunately, it was saved from demolition and reopened in the 1970s as part of the Severn Valley heritage line. On a few occasions, passengers coming into the station have seen a man and a little girl standing on the platform, wearing Edwardian costume and waving at the trains. They have taken them to be dressed that way to add a little historical flavour to the experience. According to Allan Scott-Davies, however, they are apparitions from the original days of steam. Who they are or why they haunt the station, nobody knows.

A disused railway tunnel runs under the town and this too is said to be haunted by an enigmatic ghost. It is described as 'a brightly coloured figure' and is sometimes accompanied by a feeling of terror. Mr Scott-Davies believes it might be the ghost of a railway worker who was run over by a cart and killed a century or so ago, and that the strange illumination may belong to his ghostly lantern reflecting off the damp walls of the tunnel.

This is just a selection of the many ghost stories collected from Bridgnorth. I shall end with a very strange experience which took place on the outskirts of the town in the 1850s. The yarn was collected by a pioneering folklorist, Charlotte Burne, who published an important two-volume work on *Shropshire Folk-Lore* in the 1880s. A young woman was driving some friends into Bridgnorth when the horse drawing their cart suddenly stopped dead in the road. Try as she might, she could not get the animal to take another step, so she got down and had a go at leading it by the bridle. The woman had just reached up to the bridle when she was suddenly struck by an invisible force, which threw her back against a fence. Seconds later an extraordinary and terrifying apparition manifested: a gigantic hand and arm. The hand gripped the horse's neck in 'a cruel grasp' and began to choke it.

It was midday, and the clock on St Leonard's Church began to strike. At the sound of it, 'the hand slowly unclasped its hold and faded away'. The frightened party managed to get the poor horse moving again and they arrived home in a

*A ghostly couple who look like extras from* The Railway Children *are said to wave at trains coming into the station at Bridgnorth. iStock*

39

state of collapse. The horse was never fit for work again. A few days later, the young woman learnt that her aunt, who had always treated her unkindly, had died just before noon on the day of the weird event. She wondered whether the apparition had been some sort of projection of her aunt's hatred, literally reaching out to try to hurt her one last time.

## GHOSTS OF THE GRAND HOUSES

Pitchford Hall, near the village of the same name, is a splendid example of a timber-framed Tudor mansion. Dating from 1560, with 19th-century additions, it is a classic 'black and white' building and even boasts a timber-framed treehouse in the garden. A young Princess Victoria watched a hunt from this treehouse in 1832, five years before becoming queen.

The most persistent ghost of Pitchford Hall is an inexplicable smell of tobacco which sometimes wafts up from goodness knows where. It has been confidently identified as the specific brand used by a former owner, Robin Grant, although whether this is pipe tobacco or a distinctive variety of cigarillo depends upon which source you read. On at least one occasion his apparition has been seen, in a striking black and white herring-bone patterned coat with a fur collar.

Several psychics have visited Pitchford Hall and they have all claimed to have encountered dozens of spirits lurking around the place (but since it is in their interest to locate ghosts, I view their testimony with caution). One ghost none of them saw, however, was the extraordinary phantom previously seen by a cleaning lady, that of a man she described as wearing 'green armour'. Out in the grounds, the apparition of a former gamekeeper has been seen. This unfortunate gentleman decided to take his own life after being told he had inoperable cancer. He walked into the lake singing 'Jerusalem' and so drowned himself. His ghost is said to take the same watery walk, but although the mouth is open, no sound of singing is heard.

Chetwynd Hall was pulled down years ago but its deer park survives as the showground for the Newport Show. The hall and grounds were haunted by one of Shropshire's best-known ghosts, the wild and crazy Madam Pigott. Madam Pigott was wife to a former master of Chetwynd, a cruel and vicious man. This unfortunate woman died giving birth to their first child. Her husband was unmoved, saying that he didn't care so long as the baby lived, or, as he put it: 'Sometimes one must lop the root to save the branch.' Tragically, the child died, too.

After her death Madam Pigott 'came again', to use an expression popular at the time, and proved a frightening nuisance not only in the house and grounds but in the lanes bordering the estate. Sometimes she would be seen sitting in a tree, or on a bank or high wall, stroking the hair of her dead child. But if someone passed by on a horse, she would give up this peaceful activity and immediately leap down behind the rider. The startled horse would set up a gallop, hurtling through the countryside at breakneck speed, while Madam Pigott's ghost would cling on to the no less terrified rider until they happened to cross a stream. For some reason, ghosts are often prevented from passing over running water.

Eventually, Madam Pigott became such a pest that a number of parsons were called in to exorcise her. They managed to 'pray her down' so that they could squeeze her angry spirit into a bottle, and this they threw into the middle of the Chetwynd Pool on the estate. For many years Chetwynd was free of her troublesome presence but one winter the pool froze and skaters came from far and wide to enjoy the sport. The sharp edge of a skate smashed the bottle and Madam Pigott 'came again' for a second time. Twelve more parsons were assembled and they succeeded in trapping her in another bottle. This was taken far away and dropped into the Red Sea. She has not troubled the neighbourhood since.

Sir George Blount was another notable Salopian who inspired folk tales. He was the squire of Kinlet Hall who died

*Magnificent Pitchford Hall is haunted by a former owner who loved the place so much he has chosen not leave.*

in 1581 of apoplexy brought on by discovering that his daughter had married his page boy (or so the story goes). Ironically, this meant that the page boy inherited Kinlet Hall. Sir George remained furious even after death and his enraged spirit returned to plague the young couple. He'd pop up in unexpected places, terrifying the servants, and would ride up to the hall in a spectral coach. Sometimes the coach would barge through the main entrance and trundle all over the house, even over the table while the family were at dinner. This persecution from beyond the grave became so unbearable that the family demolished Kinlet Hall and built a new house in its place, hoping this would confuse the ghost into staying away.

But even this drastic plan did not end Squire Blount's unwelcome visits. Eventually he suffered Madam Pigott's fate of being 'prayed down' by parsons and trapped in a bottle. In the 19th century, a little flat bottle was found in Kinlet Church and many locals feared it was Blount's prison. Later it was recognised as having contained a chemical used in early photography and had presumably been left behind by somebody exposing a plate of the church.

An invisible horse used to make visits to Lower Hall, Beckbury. It was heard on a number of occasions, just before Christmas, outside the window. It would whinny and stamp its hooves. By the sound of them, the hooves were striking off cobbles, even though the drive had been laid with tarmac. It is thought that the ghost might have some connection with the roistering Squire Stubbs, who lived here in the 17th century, but this has never been substantiated.

A visible phantom horse gallops about on the lawn outside Wilderhope Manor, south-west of Much Wenlock. Wilderhope is a stone-built Elizabethan manor house which today serves as an unusually magnificent youth hostel. Inside, the house is haunted by a man described by one witness as 'wearing a green cloak, a brown hat with a long white plume and leather boots that reach to his thighs'. He is thought to be a former owner, Major Thomas Smallman, an ardent Royalist who enjoyed an exciting time of it during the Civil War.

When Wilderhope Manor was raided by Roundheads, Major Smallman chased after them and, after a terrific fight in which he killed several men, brought his property home again. On another occasion he was captured while carrying important documents. He managed to escape and, hotly pursued, urged his horse to leap across a wide ravine on Wenlock Edge. The poor horse plummeted to its death, but Major Smallman survived by grabbing hold of a crab apple tree and hauling himself to safety. The place where he made this prodigious bid for freedom is now called Major's Leap. The ghost of his ill-fated steed is said to haunt the place. This is probably the same animal haunting Wilderhope Manor itself.

Minsterley Hall was built in 1581 (two years before Wilderhope) and is another of the timber-framed beauties for which Shropshire is renowned. Poltergeist activity has been observed in Minsterley Hall. On one notable occasion the troublesome spook threw into the air all the crockery, cutlery, glasses and condiments that had been standing on the dinner table. Not a single item was smashed when they

*Minsterley Hall photographed in the early 1900s. A noisy poltergeist has been known to cause a nuisance here.*

hit the floor again (other than glasses dropped by startled diners) but the mess was indescribable. The entity also had the unnerving habit of thumping loudly on the windows as if marauders were trying to get in and has caused such a rumpus during the night that frightened householders have assumed the house was being ransacked by burglars.

Two of Salop's grand houses are now enjoying a much more useful life as special schools. Overley Hall, Wellington, educates young people with autism and learning difficulties. Perhaps fittingly, the ghost said to haunt the house is that of a young girl. Her identity is a mystery but she is thought to date from the Victorian period. There are no recent reports of her making an appearance and the last occasion seems to have occurred shortly after the house had been turned into a school. A member of staff saw her running out of a former pantry, wearing a white dress.

Condover Hall is one of Shropshire's most magnificent stately homes and is now, to give it its full title, a 'Residential Activity Centre for Education, Exploration and Recreation'. This classic E-shaped Elizabethan mansion certainly makes a fine backdrop for the youngsters taking part in activities here.

Its ghost story is of the 'indelible bloodstain' variety. Such tales are common in English ghost-lore and refer to a patch of blood, usually staining the spot where some cruel murder has been committed and which refuses to be washed away. In Condover Hall's case the indelible bloodstain was in the form of a gory handprint on the banisters of the main staircase. Shortly after the house was built, the Lord of the Manor was stabbed in his bed by his son. He did not die at once, however. He succeeded in staggering out of his room, and leant on the banisters calling for help. By the time his servants reached him, he was dead.

The murderous heir promptly put the blame on the family butler, John Viam. Viam was found guilty of the crime and dragged off to the scaffold. Here, moments before his death, he pronounced a curse on Condover Hall, declaring: 'Before Heaven, I am innocent, though my master's son swears me guilty and as I perish an innocent man, may those who follow my murdered Lord be cursed.'

Many believed Viam to have been innocent and the true killer found himself ostracised. He went slowly mad in the

*The main entrance into Condover Hall, where a paranormal handprint survived as a testament to a foul murder.*

house he had so badly coveted. Then a solicitor named Owen decided to reinvestigate the case and new evidence proved that on this occasion the butler did not do it. The murdered man's son was hanged and, with no more heirs available, Owen was presented with Condover Hall. The bloody handprint on the banisters remained as testament to the cowardly deed and could not be scrubbed clean. Eventually, the staircase was removed and the indelible bloodstain went with it.

## CASTLES AND OTHER NOBLE RUINS

We have already visited three haunted castles in Shropshire, those at Shrewsbury, Ludlow and Bridgnorth. There are many more.

Whittington Castle, in the north of the county, is everything anyone would wish from a medieval castle, albeit in miniature. There is a storybook-style gatehouse, walls to walk around, and it even has its original moat, still full of water and now busy with ducks and swans. Unusually, the castle is owned not by a grand family or heritage organisation, but by the local community. On the day I visited, I found teas being served and a fundraising second-hand bookshop to browse around.

A Welsh prince, Ynyr ap Cydfarch, had a castle here first but he lost it to the Norman baron Roger de Montgomery (whom we have previously met at Shrewsbury). It was then given to Sir William Peveril (Walter Scott's 'Peveril of the Peak'), who then made it more substantial. When the wars between the Welsh princes and the English crown had subsided, Whittington Castle became more of a home than a fortress and a 'pleasaunce' – a garden of the senses – was laid out here. In time, an Elizabethan house was added to the site.

The sad ghost of Whittington Castle dates from the latter period. Two little boys vanished one afternoon and, despite anxious searches for them throughout the estate, they were never seen again. Not alive, anyway. Some years later somebody entered a rarely used room in the gatehouse and decided to investigate the contents of a dusty old chest. Inside he made a grisly discovery – the mouldering skeletons of the two missing children. They had presumably become trapped inside the chest while playing hide and seek and had

*Eerie cries have been heard in the gatehouse (pictured right) of Whittington Castle.*
*iStock*

suffocated to death. Ever since the discovery, it is said, the children's pitiful cries can be heard emanating from the gatehouse.

A particularly brutal episode of the English Civil War was played out at Hopton Castle. At that time it was owned by a 'rabid Parliamentarian' and defended by a Colonel More with a company of 24 men plus two serving girls. In April 1644 it was besieged by a force of Irish Royalists. After holding out for a number of days, the castle's resources ran dry and Colonel More held a parley with the besiegers. They offered to give up the castle provided they were allowed to march away unmolested. This was agreed to. Once the men were clear of their defences, however, the Royalists went back on their word. According to a contemporary account (archaic spelling preserved):

'Mr More was seized upon and carried away prisoner, and the twenty-four souldiers tied back to back, and then some of them had their hands cut off: some with a hand, parte of an arm, and the rest cut and mangled both on hands and armes, and then all of them throwne into a muddy pit, where as often as any of them indeavoured to raise themselves out of the mud, striving to prolong their miserable lives, they were straight by these bloody villains beate down into the mud again with great stones which they hurled at them, and in this sad manner lamentably perished.'

One of the two women was also murdered, the other cruelly treated and made to walk to Brompton Castle in order to 'tell her brother Roundheads' what to expect. After these atrocities had been carried out, the Royalists blew up Hopton

*The shattered shell of Hopton Castle, haunted by soldiers who were massacred during the English Civil War.*

Castle so that it could not be used again. This explains its ruinous condition. The unquiet spirits of the betrayed soldiers are said to still haunt the location of their brutal deaths, and ghostly re-enactments of the massacre are rumoured to occur on moonlit nights.

Although technically described as 'a fortified tower house', Acton Burnell Castle has every appearance of a medieval fortress, with its massive walls and square turrets of red sandstone. It was built in the 13th century by Edward

Burnell, Lord Chancellor to Edward I, and his surname was added to the village of Acton. In the days when kings wandered round their kingdom, Parliaments were often held in out-of-the-way places. A Parliament was held at Acton Burnell in 1283, in which a law was passed granting certain guarantees to merchants. This has become known as the 'Acton Burnell statute'.

The castle remained the home of the Burnell family for centuries, until the construction of Acton Burnell Hall nearby. After they moved into the hall, the castle began to fall into disrepair. By the time of the Gothic revival at the end of the 18th century, it had become a picturesque addition to the grounds. The ruins are beautified by a tall and spreading cypress tree, hundreds of years old.

*Acton Burnell Castle, where a phantom woman has been seen and possibly photographed. iStock*

The castle is haunted by a traditional Woman in White, although on her last recorded appearance she looked rather grey. This occurred during a ghost hunt held by a group of students. They saw a grey figure standing in a doorway and one of the team succeeded in taking a photograph of it. The ghost is supposed to be of a young woman who was fatally thrown from her horse during a fox hunt.

Stokesay Castle, near Craven Arms, is arguably the finest example of a medieval fortified manor house in England. It has massive stone walls, a castellated section and another that is timber-framed with stone supports. Stokesay Castle was built in the 13th century by a wealthy wool merchant, Laurence of Ludlow, and was garrisoned with a private army to keep his riches safe. It featured briefly in the Civil War, when it was in the hands of Royalists, but they quickly abandoned it to the Parliamentarians. Although orders came to destroy it, Stokesay fortunately escaped the fate of Hopton and Bridgnorth castles and continued to be lived in until the end of the 18th century. It was rescued from falling into irreparable decay during the 19th century and thankfully then restored to the level of preservation we can enjoy today. Stokesay Castle has been a tourist attraction since the early 1900s.

During these periods of restoration, nothing has been found of the hoard of gold that tradition states is hidden somewhere in or around Stokesay. The money did not belong to Laurence of Ludlow, as one might expect, but to twin giants who lived on promontories on either side of the valley. They buried it in a huge chest in a pool that was later used to form the moat and would throw the key between them across the valley whenever they had new cash to store. Finally, the inevitable happened, and one of them made a bad throw: the key splooshed into the moat and was lost.

The distraught giants hurried away to find a locksmith and left behind a supernatural raven to guard the treasure while they were away. For some reason, they never returned and the deathless raven is said to therefore still be guarding the giants' hoard at Stokesay Castle.

A ruined castle has a certain grandeur and romance but there is something melancholy about a house in ruins, a former home once full of life now in decay. Moreton Corbet is a case in point. This gorgeous Elizabethan mansion fell into disrepair as long ago as the 18th century and was

*Stokesay Castle is an evocative reminder of the Middle Ages and has attached to it an intriguing legend. iStock*

abandoned in 1800 by the Corbet family, who moved on to Acton Reynald Hall. What remains is a shell of red sandstone and grey limestone, with tall, elegant windows – now lacking their glass, of course – and fine carving, including weird-looking heraldic beasts. Moreton Corbet is both beautiful and spooky, redolent of lives long since passed away.

Behind the house are the remains of Moreton Corbet Castle. A Saxon fort was probably on the site first but, like so many others, this was replaced by a stone castle after the Norman Conquest. Its most impressive remaining feature is of more recent date, a 16th-century gatehouse. Moreton Corbet was knocked about a bit during the Civil War but the house, in particular, was patched up again afterwards. So some might see the ruinous condition of both castle and house as evidence of the curse supposedly placed on the Corbet family during the 17th century.

In the years leading up to the Civil War, the rise in Puritanism was viewed with suspicion by most of the landed gentry. Puritans were regularly rounded up and punished for their preaching, so much of which was directed against Church and State. Sir Vincent Corbet did not share this prejudice and found himself sympathising with a local man, Paul Homeyard, who was being persecuted for his beliefs. He allowed Homeyard to stay at Moreton Corbet. Unfortunately, Homeyard became more and more outspoken and militant, making his residence at Moreton Corbet more than just an embarrassment and eventually a liability. In the end, Sir Vincent felt he had no choice but to send the Puritan packing.

For weeks Homeyard 'hid in the woods with the foxes and the owls, and in the crannies of old ruins with the rats and the jackdaws … brooding' (to quote Charles Harper's *Haunted Houses* of 1907). For some, frankly ungrateful, reason he blamed Sir Vincent Corbet for his predicament. Chancing to see him in the grounds of Moreton Corbet, Homeyard emerged out of the shrubbery and roundly denounced Sir Vincent.

'Rejoice not in thy wealth, nor in the halls of thy pride,' Homeyard declaimed, indicating the splendid mansion before them. 'They shall be a ruin and a desolation, and the snake and the eft [newt] and the adder shall be found there, and thy house shall be full of doleful creatures.'

*The remains of beautiful Moreton Corbet harbours the ghost of the man who cursed the house.*

It is Paul Homeyard's miserable-looking spirit which is said to now skulk around the ruins of Moreton Corbet, taking what cold satisfaction he can in the bare walls of the house that had once sheltered him.

Six miles north of Telford can be found Lilleshall, one of two haunted abbeys in Shropshire. Lilleshall Abbey was founded in the 12th century by a particularly austere order of Augustinian monks. The grandeur of its ruins belies the poverty of those who lived here. Unlike so many monastic houses, Lilleshall was always short of money. This truer commitment to its purpose may be the reason it escaped King Henry VIII's first round of dissolutions. When the second round came in 1538, the community at Lilleshall submitted voluntarily and handed what little they had over to the Crown.

A phantom monk is said to wander the ruins of Lilleshall Abbey, dressed in the black habit of the Augustinians. Christine McCarthy relates an extraordinary encounter with this ghost by a former custodian of the abbey, a Mr Shaw. Mr Shaw was walking his dog through the ruins, as he did most mornings, when he saw a black figure kneeling in the place the altar would originally have been. His Jack Russell's hackles rose at the sight of this stranger and the dog began to growl. As Mr Shaw approached him, the monk rose unsteadily to his feet, leaning heavily on a stout stick. He turned to face the custodian, who saw that he was very old. Mr Shaw asked the monk what he was doing in the ruins without permission and he received the enigmatic reply:

'Have you discovered the secret of Lilleshall Abbey?'

'What secret?' asked the puzzled Mr Shaw.

'You will know when the time is ripe,' said the mysterious monk. For the briefest moment, Mr Shaw was distracted by the pulling and whining of his distressed dog. He glanced down at it and then back to the stranger – but the monk had vanished.

Bloodcurdling wails and moans have been heard coming from the ruins in the evenings. According to those who have heard the phenomenon, they sound like someone being tortured, but what they actually represent no one knows. Hopefully, not the 'secret of Lilleshall Abbey', for this would imply a very dark secret indeed.

*A ghostly brother of Lilleshall Abbey holds the key to a mysterious secret.*
*iStock*

Buildwas Abbey is of similar age to Lilleshall, but was founded by the Cistercian order. A surprising event took place here in the 14th century. John Burnell, the Abbot of Buildwas, was murdered by a gang of rebellious monks headed by one Thomas Tong. After the bloody deed was committed, Tong and his unholy cronies made their escape and were never brought to justice. Burnell's angry spirit now haunts the ruins, seeking vengeance on his killers.

Buildwas is close to the Ironbridge Gorge, a World Heritage Site. Here too there are historic buildings, but of quite a different type. Ironbridge was the cradle of the Industrial Revolution and there are a number of important remnants of its busy past. The Ironbridge Gorge Museum is housed in an impressive Victorian warehouse and this is haunted by the shade of a youngster who was killed here in a tragic accident. The boy was helping to unload a barge when a wagon slipped its brakes and crushed him.

The most famous structure here – and one which is far from ruinous – is Thomas Telford's Iron Bridge, after which the entire area is named. Constructed in 1779, this was the first bridge in the world to be made entirely out of iron. It is a majestic sight spanning the Severn gorge. On misty nights, it is said, a silent barge – or 'trow' in the local lingo – is seen drifting beneath the bridge. A tall, hooded figure stands on its prow. The trow comes to a rest on the river bank and the hooded man directs other ghostly figures as they unload a grim cargo: human bodies wrapped in shrouds. They are the victims of plague, who were secretly transported out of the cities at night to be buried in quicklime.

All the properties in this chapter are open to the public.

*A former abbot was murdered in Buildwas Abbey and now haunts the ruins.*

## RURAL HAUNTS

Shropshire's lovely and varied countryside also has its hauntings. Charlotte Burne tells an amusing story, in the dialect of the witness, about a haunted pool near the village of Longnor. The White Lady who rose from the depths of the Black Pool is thought to have drowned herself in it after an unhappy love affair. She used to wander the lanes around Longnor and was blamed for causing a number of traffic accidents. On one occasion she turned up in a local pub and danced with the young men, while carefully avoiding their touch, so that they did not realise she was a ghost. Then she spoiled the gaiety somewhat by suddenly vanishing in front of everyone.

The other encounter was told by a farm servant named Hughes, who met her while crossing over a little footbridge near the Black Pool.

'I sid [saw] 'er a-cumin', an' I thinks, 'ere's a nice young wench,' he recalled. 'Well, thinks I, who she be, I'll gi'e 'er a fright. I was a young fellow then, yo know – an' I waited till 'er come up close to me, right i' the middle o' the bridge, an' I stretched out my arms, *so* – an' I clasped 'er in 'em tight – *so*. An' theer was nothin'.'

Another traditional spook, that of a headless man, formerly haunted Hampton Woods, near Ellesmere. A parson was called in to exorcise it, and in time-honoured fashion, he did so by 'praying it down' until it was tiny enough to be fastened up in a bottle. Not wanting to take any chances, the exorcist then locked it up in not one but three iron chests, each slightly larger than the other, and then buried the whole caboodle under a barn. In addition, he ordered the ghost to remain there for 99 years (which means it's probably out again now!). Sadly, the struggle and effort was too much for the parson and, having completed his task, he died from exhaustion.

Wenlock Edge is one of Shropshire's most notable landmarks, an escarpment running between Craven Arms and Much Wenlock. It is a Site of Special Scientific Interest because of the fossil-rich nature of its limestone. Jutting out from the ridge is a crag known as Ippikin's Rock, which is named after an outlaw who used to hide out in a cave at its foot. Ippikin was a knight-turned-robber who, together with his band, amassed considerable wealth from highway robbery. Their cave below the outcrop was so well concealed that the robbers lived here unmolested for years. However, a strange kind of justice caught up with Ippikin and co one fateful day when a massive chunk of limestone fell from the top of the crag and completely blocked the entrance to their hide-out, sealing them in forever. They died a long, lingering death surrounded by their ill-gotten gains.

Ever since, Ippikin's Rock has been haunted by the robber knight, who creeps about Wenlock Edge with a lantern, as if spying out further victims. It was said that if anyone was prepared to stand on the crag and call out at midnight –

> 'Ippikin! Ippkin!
> Keep away with your long chin'

*Ippikin, the 'robber knight' of Wenlock Edge, as portrayed by Cecily Peele in her Encyclopedia of British Bogies published in the 1920s.*

– his ghost would appear. Since this is the opposite of 'keeping away', I fail to understand the point of this, especially when one is told that on his appearance, Ippikin would hurl the presumptuous person to their deaths over the Edge!

The seven-mile-long hill called the Long Mynd (after the Welsh word 'mynydd' for mountain) also has a spooky reputation. One evening a man was walking over the Long Mynd down to the village of Ratlinghope (sometimes pronounced 'Ratchup') when he came across something strange in a hollow below the hill. He saw a funeral procession approaching him through the twilight. There were dozens of mourners crowding the lane and they were moving with unseemly haste. It was like he was watching a speeded-up film. In British folklore, phantom funerals like this are said to foreshadow a real funeral due to take place in the parish, but the witness did not stay long enough in Ratlinghope to find out whether this was the case. When he arrived in the village, however, he asked about what he had seen and received the laconic reply: 'Theer's allays summat to be seed about theer!'

I unearthed many interesting ghost stories from the Shropshire countryside in a journal called *Bye-gones*, which was published in Oswestry between 1871 and 1939. It is a treasure trove of quirky local history, natural history and folklore. Comments posted by a number of correspondents in 1905 highlighted a spot between Gobowen and Whittington where there was 'allays summat to be seed', too. One correspondent narrowed the haunted location down to the lane between a hamlet called Stanyards and the railway bridge just outside Whittington. He wrote:

'Within the last two years a native of Gobowen was returning home one evening from Whittington, and on passing under the bridge, was conscious of an object which accompanied him on the opposite side of the road. When he stopped it did likewise. There was no room to account for a shadow. On arriving at Pimligog Lane, the object darted up it, and gave utterance to a terrific shriek and disappeared.'

He adds: 'Close to the Stanyards is a stile known as Duckett's Stile, and it is said that, within the memory of many, a ghost appeared in the form of an enormous, large-headed dog.'

Another correspondent heard from an old woman that the ghost also took the shape of a 'headless donkey'. Weird animal ghosts appeared in a number of other places in Shropshire. A prolific correspondent to *Bye-gones*, only known by the initials 'J.E.A.', also noted:

'A spectre dog haunted the Montford Bridge side of the Grange Bank. His shape was visible, but not that of his human companion, whose presence was only made known by the sound of his footsteps. A little further on another shadowy dog was wont to frequent the neighbourhood of the gravel pit beyond Ensdon House, and the turn of Felton Butler. Another such ghost kept guard on the hilly road above Clun, on the way to Knighton.'

Even weirder spooks were associated with Weston Bridge at Worthen, according to J.E.A. On 8 July 1903, he wrote that the spectres manifested in a number of 'uncanny shapes', including 'an army of immense rats'!

A few months later, he wrote in with another tradition attached to the area: 'The legend I heard in connection with this bridge was that years ago a man was killed in a field close by. He was either riding and was thrown from his horse, or else was at work and was killed by means of a horse. At all events his death was caused by a horse; and ever after (or till recent times) noises of invisible horses galloping and neighing were to be heard in the night-time at this bridge.'

*A man walking over the Long Mynd one evening encountered a spectral funeral cortege. iStock*

As we have seen before, for example at the Major's Leap and Wilderhope Manor, phantom horses are common in Shropshire ghost-lore. A vivid account of such a ghost is also to be found in the pages of the 1903 edition of *Bye-gones*, this time presented by a correspondent calling him or herself 'M.A.P.' The story was told to M.A.P. by a close relative:

'In the days long before the Llanymynech bridge over the Virniew [Vyrnwy] was built,' writes M.A.P., 'there was somewhere in its neighbourhood a forge, and the road beyond the river was lined on each side by a wood, making it after dark a gloomy spot. This part of the road was said to be haunted by a white horse, bridled and saddled, but riderless, which galloped furiously along the dark road from the ford, and upon its shoulders it bore great blood clots.

'In her early youth my relative went on Wednesday to Oswestry market to make the usual purchases, and rode rather a spirited young horse, with a pannier upon the offside. Upon one particular Wednesday she was much delayed, having more purchases to make than usual, and she returned loaded, the pannier being full, and carried beside over her left arm a bag. She was most anxious to cross over the ford on her return before dark, being made timid by the stories she had heard, but night had set in before she came to it. Loaded as she was, she dreaded the crossing, and it was with difficulty she got her steed to enter the water, but when she had crossed, the spirited animal, smelling his stable, set off at a sharp canter.

'While she was incommoded by her load and the pulling of the horse, she distinctly heard behind her the terrifying sound of a furious galloping, and her steed, appearing to hear it also, set off furiously in the pitch darkness, and to her horror, glancing behind, she saw coming on at her flank the outstretched head and neck of the white horse. She was now near to the end of the wood, and as she emerged, the sound of the spectre ceased, but her own animal raced on, only stopping at the gate of the farm, and backing to permit her to open it, then raced for home, where he stood in the farmyard trembling with fear.'

*The River Vyrnwy near Llanymynech. A phantom horse has been known to gallop furiously on a wood-bound lane beyond the river. iStock*

Unfortunately, no tradition was recorded to explain the existence of the spectral steed with the blood clots on its shoulders. Presumably it was still galloping after its rider had been struck from its saddle during some long-forgotten battle or incidence of highway robbery. Dramatic story though this is, it cannot compare with the remarkable animal-like ghost we will encounter next.

## THE ROARING BULL

The legend of the 'Roaring Bull of Bagbury' tells of a bizarre and terrifying apparition: a huge, bellowing bull without any skin, a gory and horrible monstrosity. Bagbury is a village near the border with Powys. A local farmer named Hayward gave one account of the Roaring Bull to *Shropshire Folk-Lore* author Charlotte Burne. He told her:

'There was a very bad man lived at Bagbury Farm, and when he died it was said that he had never done but two good things in his life, and the one was to give a waistcoat to a poor old man, and the other was to give a piece of bread and cheese to a poor boy, and when the man died he made a sort of confession of this. But when he was dead his ghost would not rest, and he would get in the [farm] buildings in the shape of a bull, and roar till the boards and the shutters and the tiles would fly off the building, and it was impossible for anyone to live near him. He never come till about nine or ten at night, but he got so rude at last that he would come about seven or eight at night, and he was so troublesome that they sent for twelve parsons to lay him.

*The little bridge below which the terrifying Roaring Bull of Bagbury
was imprisoned. © Richard Holland*

'And the parsons came, and they got him under, but they could not lay him; but they got him, in the shape of a bull all the time, up into Hyssington Church [just over the Welsh border]. And when they got him into the church, they all had candles, and one old blind parson, who knowed him and who knowed what a rush he would make, he carried his candle in his top boot. And he made a great rush, and all the candles went out, all but the blind parson's, and he said, "You light your candles by mine." And while they were in the church, before they laid him, the bull made such a burst that he cracked the wall of the church from the top to the bottom, and the crack was left as it was for years, till the church was done up; it was left on purpose for people to see. I've seen it hundreds of times.

'Well, they got the bull down at last, into a snuff-box, and he asked them to lay him under Bagbury Bridge, and that every mare that passed over should lose her foal and every woman her child; but they would not do this, and they laid him in the Red Sea for a thousand years.'

Other accounts make it quite clear that the Roaring Bull is indeed laid under Bagbury Bridge. Even Mr Hayward seems to confirm this. He said: 'Folk were always frightened to go over Bagbury Bridge. I've been over it myself many times with horses, and I always got off the horse and made him go quietly, and went pit-pat, ever so softly for fear of him hearing me and coming out.'

There is something darkly pagan about the image of this monstrous bull. It is tempting to see it as a folk memory of some totemic animal from the dim and distant past, later demonised in the imaginations of the people. Wild bulls certainly lived in the British Isles in prehistoric times and were considerably bigger and fiercer than the maddest bull you might find in a farmyard today. It's not unreasonable to suppose that such an animal would have significance for our ancient ancestors.

Remarkably, the Bagbury Bull is not unique in Shropshire ghost-lore. Charlotte Burne learnt of another example from an elderly resident of Millichope. He told her that centuries before, a squire of Millichope Hall met his death after falling from an upper-storey window. Presumably this was no accident, for one of the results of his demise was a bloodstain that refused to be washed away. As we know, indelible bloodstains like this one usually point to a murder having been committed. So, perhaps this was no accident and the squire was in fact pushed out of the window.

After the suspicious death, the estate passed to the wrong heir – suggesting this was indeed a case of murder – and the squire's restless spirit began to haunt the neighbourhood of Millichope Hall. However, he did not 'come again' in his own form, but in the appearance of 'a flayed bull'.

*Spectral bulls are a feature of Shropshire ghost-lore. iStock*

## THE LEGEND OF WILD EDRIC

Our final story from the Shropshire countryside dates back more than 800 years. It is an intriguing blend of ghost-lore and fairy-lore and, despite being written down in the 12th century, was still remembered and talked about by rural Salopians into the 20th.

'Wild' Edric Salvage is recorded in the Domesday Book of 1086 as an Anglo-Saxon who owned extensive estates in Shropshire and Herefordshire. He resisted the Norman Conquest for a number of years but soon saw which side his bread was best buttered on and made peace with William I. Some years later, however, he attempted to throw off the Norman yoke and his estates were forfeited. He seems to have become something of a guerrilla leader after that but his eventual fate is not known.

In the following century, the historian Walter Map set down a strange story about Edric in his book *De Nugis Curialium* ('Trifles of Courtiers'), first published in about the year 1180. One day, according to Map, Edric became lost in the forest of Clun while out hunting. After wandering around for hours, he saw a light shining through the trees. He made his way towards it and came across a building in the depths of the woods. Peering through a window, he watched in wonder as a number of beautiful, stately women danced in a circle. One in particular attracted him. He burst his way in, grabbed the girl who had taken his fancy and carried her away before anyone could stop him.

Somehow Edric found his way back to his court, his captive in tow. The woman's beauty captivated everyone but she refused to speak for three days and nights. Then she relented and told Edric she was prepared to marry him, on the condition that he allowed her to return to the forest to meet her sisters when she felt like it and that he should never reproach her for doing so. If he broke this promise, she warned him, she would instantly leave him and calamity would come upon him. Edric agreed and he and the lovely woman from the woods were married. For many years they lived in harmony together and Edric showed no jealousy over his wife's regular visits to her sisters. One fateful day, however, he returned from hunting to find the house empty. By the time his wife eventually returned, Edric was in a foul temper.

*The Shropshire countryside seen through a window of ruined Clun Castle. At the time of Edric Salvage the land around Clun was mainly forest, in the depths of which he is said to have found a bride in mysterious circumstances. iStock*

'I suppose it was those sisters of yours who kept you so long?' he growled. That was enough. The injunction had been broken. His wife vanished in the wink of an eye and though he searched and searched, Edric found neither his wife nor the mysterious building in the woods again. He became ill and listless, he lost his home and his estates and died of despair.

So ends the story as set down by Walter Map. It represents a fairly common type of folk tale in which a fairy bride is captured and married under certain conditions, which are inevitably broken. In Wales such stories usually involved never touching the women with iron (which is inimical to fairy folk), while in the Scottish isles a Seal Maiden would only remain with her mortal husband so long as he was able to keep her seal skin hidden from her. There is considerable evidence, especially from the earliest recorded fairy tales dating back to the Early Middle Ages, that fairies were actually perceived as spirits of the dead. This is certainly true of another story told by Walter Map, in which a man sees his recently deceased wife dancing in similar circumstances to those observed by Edric Salvage.

Locally, Edric became something of a folk hero, in the King Arthur mould. One legend had it that he and his wife and all his court were sleeping underground, waiting for England to be restored to a time resembling the nation he knew, before the Norman Conquest. He would wake occasionally to knock on the walls of lead mines to indicate to the miners where rich seams could be found.

More popular, however, were the accounts of 'Wild Edric' and his courtiers riding pell-mell through the moonlit countryside. Their favourite stamping ground was over the county's distinctive ridge of quartzite tors, the Stiperstones. Edric's queen, Godda, would rejoin him for these nocturnal rides. Their appearance was considered to be an omen of forthcoming war. Witnesses told Victorian folklorist Charlotte Burne that Wild Edric and company were seen to ride just prior to the Napoleonic and the Crimean wars.

*The Stiperstones, where Wild Edric, Queen Godda and their ghostly courtiers would be seen riding whenever war threatened the nation. iStock*

Later accounts refer to appearances months before the outbreak of the two world wars, proving the persistence of Wild Edric's legend.

One of the witnesses stated that 'Edric had short dark curly hair and very bright black eyes'. She continued: 'He wore a green cap and white feather, a short green coat and cloak, a horn and a short sword hanging from his golden belt. The lady had wavy golden hair falling loosely to her waist, and round her forehead a band of white linen, with a golden ornament in it. The rest of her dress was green, and she had a short dagger at her waist.'

Their green clothing is another link with fairy tradition, for fairies were popularly believed to wear green. Here Edric and Godda are taking the place of the Wild Hunt, an Anglo-Saxon and Norse superstition, remnants of which survive throughout Britain. Elsewhere the master of the Wild Hunt is the Devil, the god Woden or some fiendish individual belonging to a particular region. Sometimes devilish hounds would accompany the hunt, seeking wicked souls to devour.

*A Victorian representation of the Wild Hunt, a phenomenon represented in Shropshire by Wild Edric and his ghostly courtiers.*

## OUT NOW

**BLACK COUNTRY & BIRMINGHAM** Ghost Stories
**CAMBRIDGESHIRE** Ghost Stories
**CHESHIRE** Ghost Stories
**CORNISH** Ghost Stories
**COTSWOLDS** Ghost Stories
**CUMBRIAN** Ghost Stories
**DERBYSHIRE** Ghost Stories
**ESSEX** Ghost Stories
**KENT** Ghost Stories
**LANCASHIRE** Ghost Stories
**LEICESTERSHIRE** Ghost Stories
**LONDON** Ghost Stories
**LONDON UNDERGROUND** Ghost Stories
**NORTH WALES** Ghost Stories
**OXFORDSHIRE** Ghost Stories
**SCOTTISH** Ghost Stories
**SOUTH WALES** Ghost Stories
**STAFFORDSHIRE** Ghost Stories
**SURREY** Ghost Stories
**SUSSEX** Ghost Stories
**WELSH CELEBRITY** Ghost Stories
**YORKSHIRE** Ghost Stories

### Coming In 2015

**DORSET** Ghost Stories
**HEREFORDSHIRE** Ghost Stories
**NORFOLK** Ghost Stories
**SOMERSET** Ghost Stories
**WARWICKSHIRE** Ghost Stories
**WILTSHIRE** Ghost Stories

### Coming In 2016

**NORTHUMBERLAND** Ghost Stories
**NOTTINGHAMSHIRE** Ghost Stories
**DEVON** Ghost Stories
**LINCOLNSHIRE** Ghost Stories

BRADWELL
**BOOKS**

See website for more details: **www.bradwellbooks.co.uk**